BEADWORK®

Creates

Beaded
Beads

*Edited by
Jean
Campbell*

INTERWEAVE PRESS

Printed and bound in China by Asia Pacific

Library of Congress Cataloging-in-Publication Data

Beadwork creates beaded beads : 30 designs / Jean Campbell, editor.
  p. cm.
 ISBN 1-931499-27-6
1. Beadwork. 2. Jewelry making. I. Campbell, Jean, 1964-   .
 TT860 .B335 2003
 745.58'2--dc21

                                  2002151327

10 9 8 7 6 5 4 3 2 1

Project editor: Jean Campbell
Technical editor: Dustin Wedekind
Illustrations: Ann Swanson
Photography: Joe Coca
Book design: Paulette Livers
Photo styling: Leigh Radford and Linda Ligon
Book production: Samantha Thaler
Proofreader: Nancy Arndt

Interweave Press
201 East Fourth Street
Loveland, Colorado
80537-5655 USA
www.interweave.com

Dear Reader,

What is a beaded bead? I heard that question a lot when I was putting this book together. Here's my answer: "It's a bead covered with beads or one made solely out of beads, like a miniature sculpture with a hole in it. You can wear it alone on a chain or incorporate it into elaborate pieces of jewelry. Some beaded beads are suave, some are spunky, some are just plain beautiful. They work up quickly and are much like potato chips—you can't make just one." My explanation often received blank stares until I displayed a sample of the real thing. So the main point is this: Beaded beads are as varied as their makers. They are versatile components for jewelry-making, and they're just about as instantly gratifying as beadwork gets.

Before you start on your own beaded beads, be sure to check the Tips section on page 104. Another resource is the Stitches section on page 105, which clearly defines each stitch used in the book. Together, the illustrations and words will help you learn a new stitch or jog your bead-stitching memory.

Now's the time for fun! Page through these thirty wonderful projects, pick a favorite beaded bead, rummage through your stash, and make one—after another, after another, after another. Don't worry, they're not fattening!

—Jean Campbell
Editor, *Beadwork*
magazine and books

Con

tents

Santa Fe

Linda Richmond

Make this lovely little bead in under an hour. Make a whole bunch and use them as components in a necklace or bracelet.

Materials
Orange, green, navy, light blue, light purple, dark purple, and silver Delica beads
Two 7mm–8mm beads
Size D beading thread

Notions
Size 12 beading or sharps needles
Scissors
Beeswax

Step 1: Using a yard of double and waxed thread and leaving a 4" tail, follow the chart inside the black lines with flat peyote stitch. When you are through, fold the jagged ends of the beadwork together. Use a zigzag path to sew them together, locking the beads like a zipper. Put a needle on your tail thread and use this thread to connect the adjoining beads. Continue through several more beads and trim the tail close to the work.

Step 2: Your working thread should exit from one of the beads at the end. Stand the tube on end with your thread exiting the top. Use orange Delicas to work a round of brick stitch. Begin the round by stringing two beads, passing under the loop of thread between the peyote-stitched beads, and back through the second bead just strung. Snug the beads tight. Continue around, adding one bead at time. Finish the round by passing down through the first bead added in this step.

Pass through several beads to secure the thread and trim close to work.

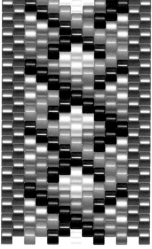

Step 3: Use larger beads to fill the inside of the tube. They will firm up and strengthen your beaded bead. Use beads that measure as close as possible to the inside diameter of your tube. Fill the beaded bead by stringing the filler beads first and then sliding the beaded bead over them. Don't let these larger beads completely fill the tube from end-to-end because the beads you string on either side of the beaded beads usually need to be able to sit a little bit inside the beaded beads. No need to worry about the color of the filler beads since they will be hidden.

Linda Richmond lives in Sandpoint, Idaho, and has been captivated by beads for most of her life. She launched a full-time beading career in 1995. She now sells her kits, along with beads, tools, books, and supplies, through her website at www.lindarichmond.com.

Golden Gumdrops

Nancy Zellers

Resin beads come in the most delicious colors and look like a bag of gumdrops, ready to be gobbled up. How to make them even more luscious? Cover them with golden crystal seed beads using right-angle weave.

Materials
18mm–20mm resin bead
Size 15° silver-lined gold beads
Size B beading thread to match the resin bead
Double-faced transparent tape
Masking tape

Notions
Size 10 or 12 beading or sharps needle
Scissors
Thread Heaven
Wooden skewer

Step 1: Make a strip of right-angle weave two units wide and as long as necessary to go around the resin bead. Leave a space for one last unit.

Step 2: Cut a strip of tape in half lengthwise and stick it to the bead's circumference. Place your beaded strip over the tape. Weave the last unit, connecting the beginning and the end of the strip.

Step 3: Weave through beads to the top of the strip. Start a new round of right-angle weave on any of the beads along the edge of the strip. Work right-angle weave around the strip, decreasing as needed to keep the seed beads flush to the resin bead. When you reach the starting point on the round, it will take just one bead to complete the last unit. Weave to the top of this round to begin the next round.

Step 4: Continue working the rounds, making decreases as necessary, usually one or more per round. Your last round near the hole will have a decrease in every unit.

Step 5: Pass through the top bead of each unit and pull snug to make a ring around the hole. Pass through the ring several times to strengthen the connection and secure the thread. Weave through the beads so that you exit from a bead at the bottom of the initial strip.

Step 6: Insert a skewer through the resin bead from the beaded side. The skewer will prevent the beads from sliding as you work, keeping the holes aligned. Wrap the skewer with masking tape to help it fit.

Step 7: Repeat Steps 3–5 to cover the other half of the bead. Remove the double-faced tape from the resin bead after you complete the first round of the second half. After you complete all of the right-angle weave, trim the working thread close to the work.

Nancy Zellers lives in Aurora, Colorado, and enjoys making simple yet elegant beaded jewelry. Nancy has kits available. Contact her at spsnoz2276@aol.com.

Ruffled Net

Barbara L. Grainger

Unusual and contrasting color combinations accentuate the structure of this fun and funky bead. Begin with a netted tube, then work rounds of increased netting on each end for a ruffled extravaganza.

Materials
Size 11° seed beads in two colors (A and B)
Size B beading thread in color to complement beads

Notions
Size 12 beading needle
Scissors

Round 1: Using 3' of thread and leaving a 4" tail, string 12 A. Tie into a circle.

Round 2: *String 3 A. Skip 3 beads on the circle and pass through the next. Repeat from * twice to make three nets. Then pass through the first two beads added in this round.

Rounds 3–5: *String 3 A and pass through the middle bead of the next net. Repeat from * twice to make three nets. Then pass through the first two beads added in this round.

Round 6: Repeat Round 5, except after the last net pass through the first bead added in this round.

Round 7: Make increases by *stringing 3 A. Skip the middle bead of the first net of the previous round and pass through the third bead of the same net. String 3 A. Pass through the first bead of the next net. Repeat from * twice for a total of 6 nets. Then pass through the first two beads added in this round (Figure 1).

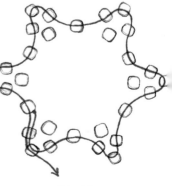

Figure 1

Round 8: *String 3 A and pass through the middle bead of the next net in the previous round. Repeat from * all around to make 6 nets (Figure 2). Then pass through the first bead added in this round.

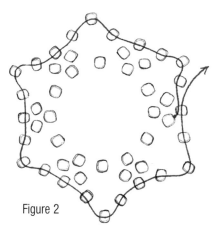

Figure 2

Round 9: Make increases by *stringing 3 A. Skip the middle bead of the first net the previous round and pass through the third bead of the same net. String 3 A. Pass through the first bead of the next net. Repeat from * to the end of the round for a total of 12 nets. Then pass through the first two beads added in this round.

Round 10: *String 3 A and pass through the middle bead of the next net in the previous round. Repeat from * all around to make twelve 12 nets. Then pass through the first bead added in this round.

Round 11: Make increases by *stringing 3 A. Skip the middle bead of the first net of the previous round and pass through the third bead of the same net. String 3 A. Pass through the first bead of the next net. Repeat from * to the end of the round for a total of 24 nets. Then pass through the first two beads added in this round.

16

Round 12: *String 3 A and pass through the middle bead of the next net in the previous round. Repeat from * all around to make 24 nets. Then pass through the first two beads added in this round.

Round 13: Make increases by *stringing 3 B. Skip the middle bead of the first net of the previous round and pass through the third bead of the same net. String 3 A. Pass through the first bead of the next net. Repeat from * to the end of the round for a total of 48 nets.

Secure your thread by tying a knot between beads and passing through several more. Begin a new thread at Round 1 and exit from the first bead of a net. Repeat Rounds 7–13 to make the other end of the beaded bead. Tie a knot between beads and/or weave your thread through several beads to secure. Trim thread close to the work.

Barbara L. Grainger is an internationally recognized beadwork author, instructor, and designer who specializes in innovative beadwork techniques.

Simple Wrap

Diane Fitzgerald

This is the easiest of beaded beads, and it works great in a loop and button beaded clasp. Also don't underestimate its power to use in a simple necklace, or as a fringe element on a purse, a bracelet, or a lampshade.

Materials
8mm round base bead
Size 11° seed beads
Size D beading thread

Notions
Size 12 beading needle
Scissors

Step 1: Using a yard of thread and leaving a 4" tail, pass up through the hole of the base bead. Knot working thread to the tail. Position knot at the top of the bead.

Step 2: String 8 seed beads or enough beads to run from the top of the base bead to the bottom of your base bead. Holding your seed beads in place, pass up through the base bead (Figure 1).

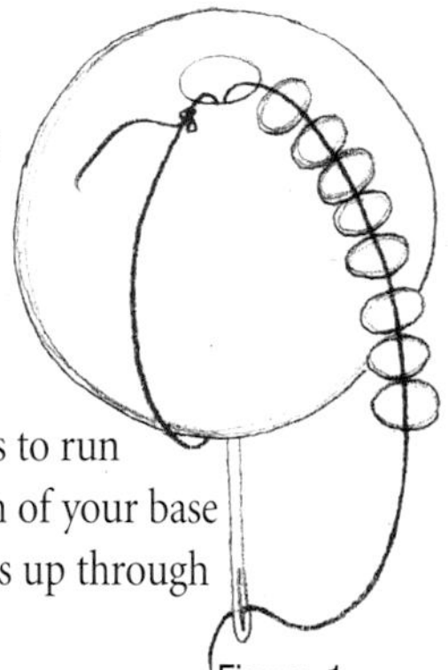

Figure 1

Step 3: Pass down through the first bead of the first strand. String 6 seed beads or 2 less than you used in Step 2. Pass through the last bead added on the previous strand (Figure 2) and through the base bead.

Step 4: Repeat Steps 2 and 3 seven more times. Tie a knot between beads, pass through several more seed beads, and trim the thread close to the work.

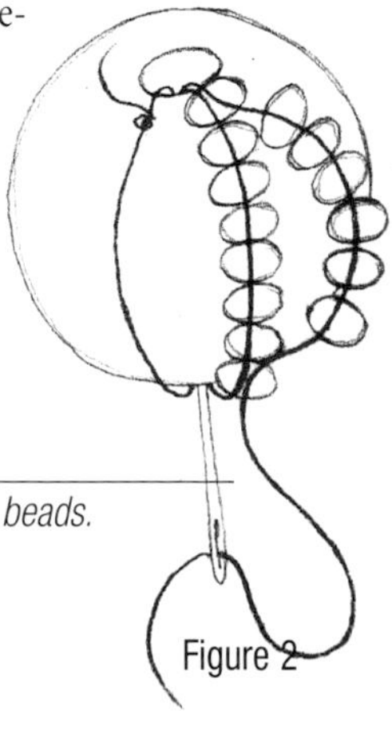

Like many of us, Diane Fitzgerald is addicted to beads. You may reach her at dmfbeads@bitstream.net.

Figure 2

Sculpturally Yours

Judi Wood

This peyote beaded bead adds pizzazz to an otherwise plain necklace. Also use it as the special accent for a bracelet or earring, or even as a spectacular clasp bead. There's no need to follow a pattern—just follow your heart! If you don't feel ready to experiment with color, experiment with bead sizes and types instead.

Materials
5mm or larger wood or plastic large-holed bead
Size 11° Japanese seed beads
Size 14° Japanese seed beads
Charlottes
Nailheads, small rice or seed pearls, 3mm crystal or fire-polished beads
Size B beading thread in color to complement beads

Notions
Size 12 English or size 16 Japanese beading needle
Sharp scissors
Thread conditioner or beeswax

Step 1: Using a yard of thread and leaving a 4" tail, pass through the wooden bead's hole and tie a knot. String an even amount of two colors of size 11's that can wrap around the circumference of the wood bead. Pass through all the beads just strung (Figure 1).

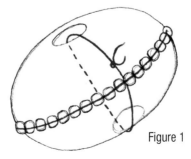

Figure 1

Step 2: Work one-drop peyote off one side of the ring. Make decreases as needed for the size of the bead you are covering. Some core beads need immediate decreases while others can wait for several rounds. Make a decrease when the space between 2 size 11°s is smaller than a size 11°, or the beads start to lean toward each other. If you make one decrease, be sure to make other decreases at least two or three more spots in the same round.

Make a decrease by passing through a space where you would regularly add a size 11°. You can also make a decrease by adding a charlotte or size 14°.

Step 3: In rounds following decreases, stitch a nailhead, pearl, crystal, or fire-polished bead over the decreases from the previous round. This embellishment will cover the space perfectly.

Step 4: In the rounds following the addition of the larger beads, work as though the larger beads are just a natural part of the peyote-stitched round.

Step 5: Work the subsequent rounds with size 11°s, using decreases as necessary. You will probably need to work two or three size 11°s in the space above the larger beads.

Step 6: Work the other side of the bead following Steps 2–5 until each side of the bead is covered; leave the hole on each side of the core bead open. After completing the last round pass through all the beads added in the last two rounds and through several beads on the next three or four rounds.

Step 7: Using the peyote stitch on the core bead as a base, begin another layer of peyote stitch with charlottes and size 14°s. Work the beads between the peyote-stitched rounds on the base. Do so by stringing a bead and stitching into the next bead on the base, stringing a bead and stitching into the next bead on the base. This technique creates a dimensional effect for the bead. There is no set amount of beads that need to be added, just work the bead until the look pleases you.

Award winning artist Judi Wood is a frequent contributor to Beadwork *magazine. Find her work and show information at www.JudiWood.com.*

Right-Angle Weave Tubes

Mary Tafoya

Challenge yourself with interesting patterns and color combinations as you create this simple yet elegant right-angle woven bead.

Materials
Bone hairpipe or any long, gently tapered bead
Size 11° Japanese seed beads
Size 14° Japanese seed beads
Size B beading thread in color to complement beads

Notions
Size 12 beading needle
Scissors
Thread Heaven thread conditioner

Step 1: Using 4' of conditioned thread and leaving a 2' tail, string 8 size 11's and tie them in a circle. Pass through the first two beads to move away from the knot.

Step 2: String 6 size 11's and pass through the first and second beads to form a second unit. Reinforce the second unit by making a figure-eight thread path (Figure 1). Do so by passing through the first unit and then through the ninth, tenth, eleventh, and twelfth beads just added.

Figure 1

Continue working right-angle weave and reinforcing the units until you have a strip that will wrap snugly around the circumference of the base bead.

Step 3: String 2 size 11's and pass through the two available side beads from the first unit of the strip. Reinforce them by passing through the first unit and exit from the two side beads you first entered. String 2 size 11's and reinforce them by passing through the last unit of the strip. Reinforce again, if necessary. Weave through the beads so you exit from the beads at the side of a unit from the first round.

Step 4: Keep the beadwork on the base bead as you work the subsequent rounds. Begin the second round by stringing 6 size 11's and passing through the side of the unit you exited from in the first round. Pass through the first four beads just added. Continue around the base bead, adding four beads at a time to make the right-angle weave units. String 2 size 11's to complete the last unit of the round. Reinforce, and exit from the beads at the side of a unit from the second round.

Repeat this step to cover the rest of the base bead. Once your bead count no longer fits tightly around the base bead, switch to size 14's.

Step 5: Finish the first half of the right-angle weave work by reinforcing the side beads of the last round. Pass straight through all those beads four times. Weave through several beads on the body of the beadwork and trim the thread close to the work.

Step 6: Thread a needle on the tail thread and repeat Steps 4 and 5 to completely cover the bead.

Mary Tafoya lives and beads in Albuquerque, New Mexico, and is a regular contributor to Beadwork. *Visit Mary's website at http://www.flash.net/~mjtafoya.*

Sparkly Wheels

Nikia Angel

These sparkly donuts will get your wheels moving! Once you've mastered the basic bead, experiment by mixing bead types, shapes, and colors. They look great all strung together or alone on a single chain.

Materials
4mm Austrian crystals or 4mm fire-polished beads
Delicas or size 15° seed beads
Size B beading thread in color to complement beads

Notions
Scissors
Beeswax

Step 1: Using 3' of thread and leaving a 4" tail, *string 1 crystal and 1 Delica. Repeat from * nine times. Pass through all the beads again, exiting from the last bead strung. Tie a square knot to make a foundation circle.

Step 2: Pass through the next crystal and Delica. *String 5 Delicas. Skip over the next crystal on the foundation circle and pass through the next Delica. Repeat from * around to make a series of nets (Figure 1).

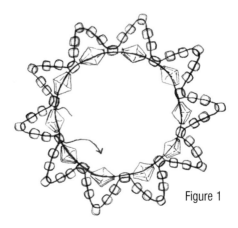

Figure 1

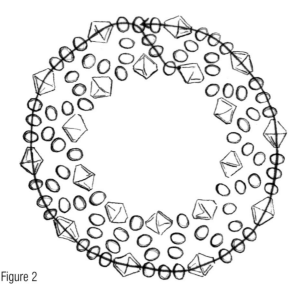

Figure 2

Step 3: Weave through the beads so you exit from the center bead of one of the nets created in Step 2. *String 1 Delica, 1 crystal, 1 Delica. Pass through the middle bead of the next net. Repeat from * all around (Figure 2). Pull your thread tight and pass through the beads added in this step again, exiting from the middle Delica of a net created in Step 2.

Step 4: *String 5 Delicas. Skip over the next Delica, crystal, and Delica added in Step 3 and pass through the next Delica. Repeat from * around to make another series of nets. Continue to pull tight. Exit from the middle bead of one of the nets.

Step 5: *String 1 crystal. Pass through the middle bead of the next net created in Step 4. Pull tight. Repeat from * all around. Secure your working and tail threads by weaving the thread through several beads, making a knot between beads, passing through more beads to hide the knot, and trimming the thread close to the work.

Nikia Angel has been beading obsessively for over fifteen years. When not in her bead room surrounded by beads she is at work managing a bead store in Albuquerque and trying to "hook" new beaders.

Cubies

Chris Prussing

These cute little beads employ a clever use of right-angle weave. String them together for an interesting piece of jewelry or just keep them separate for stacking and sorting—a great stress reliever!

Materials
Size 10° seed beads in three colors
Size 11° seed beads
3 yards of Power Pro #10 test

Notions
2 size 10 beading needles
2 size 12 beading needles
Scissors

Note: I recommend two-needle right-angle weave. Single-needle right-angle weave can also be used, but you'll need about a third more thread, and you may need to use a thinner thread than Power Pro.

Step 1: Using 2 yards of thread and size 10's, make a 19-unit by 5-unit right-angle weave mat. Begin the mat in the lower left and end in the upper right. Follow the chart bead color placement (Figure 1).

Step 2: Put the ends of the mat together and pinch it into a square so it stands upright as an open box. Continue the right angle weave to connect the ends of the mat.

Step 3: Weave to the closest side bead on the mat and work right-angle weave across the bottom of the open cube, attaching all

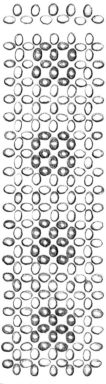

Figure 1

four sides. Turn the cube so that your working thread is on the bottom in the southeast corner.

Step 4: Begin a new 1-yard thread on the top of the cube in the upper southeast corner. Right-angle weave across the top as you did the bottom. Your bottom and top threads should end up in opposite corners of the cube.

Step 5: Use a size 10° to sew into the first corner. Continue across one top edge and add size 11's between the edge right-angle woven beads to reinforce (Figure 2), and size 10's at the corners. Continue around the top and bottom perimeters, using the top thread for the top edges, the bottom thread for the bottom edges.

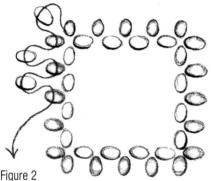
Figure 2

Step 6: Using size 12 needles, sew size 11° reinforcing beads down the two opposite sides. Do so by weaving through the top and bottom edges that have already been reinforced, and through the corner beads as well.

If using two needles, tie a square knot and stitch the thread ends in opposite directions through adjacent beads. Then pull one thread end to reposition the knot inside a bead. Tighten the knot, stitch the ends through a few more beads, and trim close to the work. You may also tie a knot between beads, weave through several beads to hide the knot, pass through a few more, and trim all threads close to the work.

Chris Prussing is a bead artist who can be contacted at www.rightangleweave.com.

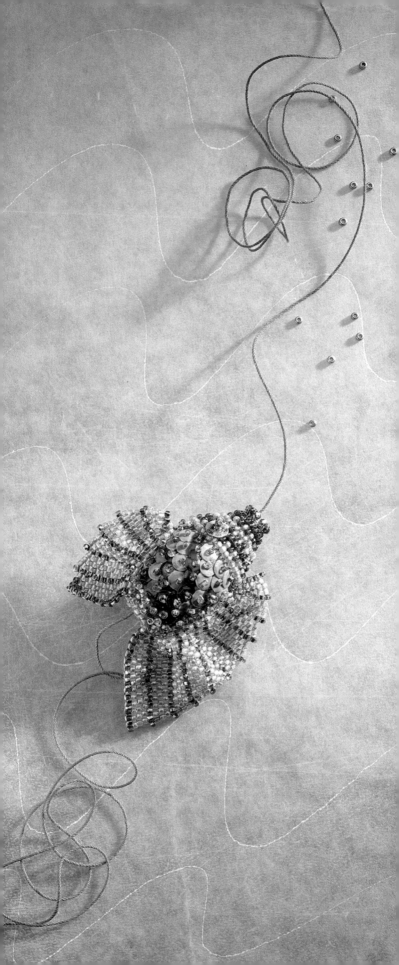

Here Fishy, Fishy, Fishy

Dustin Wedekind

A fishing float is the perfect form for a beaded fish. Select one that has a hollow sliding plug running down its length so you can use the plug to string the bead when it's completed. Be sure that the plug is tight and sticks out slightly at both ends. You may glue the plug in place if it is loose.

Materials
1½" fish float
3mm–5mm sequins
Size 11° and 15° seed beads in golds and greens
Knit fabric in color coordinating with beads and sequins
Size B beading thread

Notions
Beading needle
Scissors
Super Glue
Toothpick

BODY
Step 1: Cover the float with fabric by cutting the fabric to size and sewing the ends together. The sewing doesn't have to be very neat, but it should be as tight and smooth as possible.

Step 2: Backstitch a row of green size 11°s around the back opening (the end that has less plug sticking out). Stitch a row of green along the top of the float, from the back to about halfway to the front. Stitch another row along the bottom, from the back to about two-thirds to the front (Figure 1). These rows will be the foundations for the fins.

Note: Begin and end your thread by tying knots in the fabric. You can maneuver the needle and thread around by passing under the fabric.

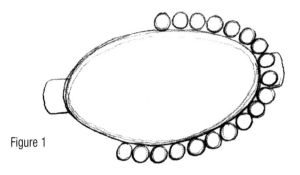

Figure 1

Step 3: Bring the needle out of the fabric a half-sequin distance from the ring of beads. *String a 3mm sequin and a size 15°. Pass back through the sequin and exit the fabric next to the sequin. Repeat from * all around the bead, overlapping the sequins and not putting sequins over the size 11° rows. Stitch another row with 3mm sequins, overlapping the previous row. After two or three rows, switch to 5mm sequins. The larger sequins look more like scales and using a mixture of colors helps define the scale pattern. Work rows of sequins up to the end of the longer line of size 11's.

Step 4: Backstitch a row of gold size 11's around the front opening of the bead. Square-stitch a row of beads on top of the back-stitched beads to cover the plug and form the fish's lips.

Step 5: Backstitch rows of green size 11's starting around the lips and working toward the sequins. Add more sequins or beads to cover the fabric where the sequins and the beads meet.

FINS

Step 6: Begin a new thread at one end of a size 11° row. Work peyote stitch by passing through the first bead and stringing 1 gold size 11°. Pass through the third bead and string another gold size 11°. Repeat to the end of the row. Work back the other direction, adding 2 green between each gold. Work back, adding a gold above each gold and a green between each green.

Step 7: Work the rest of the fin without increasing the peyote stitches, with 3 green between lines of gold. After 4 to 5 rows, begin decreasing by passing back through two rows at the front of the fin, and continue building the back side of the fin (Figure 2). Work until the decreases meet up with the back of the fin.

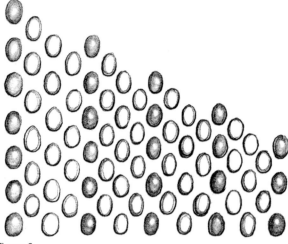

Figure 2

Repeat from Step 6 for the other fin. The bottom fin will be larger because the stitched base row is longer. The larger fin will serve as ballast to make the fish hang right-side-up.

Step 8: Make two eyes with gold sequins and green size 11's on top of the beads at the front of the fish.

Step 9: Use a toothpick to dab each beaded sequin with super glue as a snagging precaution. The smell will go away in a day or two.

Dustin Wedekind is the managing editor of Beadwork.

Fandango

Jeannette Cook

Create these fanciful brick-stitched beads using a variety of bead sizes, shapes, and colors. Since you'll be beading over a plastic tube, experiment with its height and width to get a variety of looks. The bead sequence in the instructions is just a suggestion—play with different combinations to come up with something completely new!

Materials

Assorted shapes, sizes, and colors of beads
  (size 6°–11° seeds, cubes, twisted hex, etc.)
Tiny plastic bead storage tube
Size D Nymo beading thread to complement beads

Notions

2 size 12 needles
Scissors

BASIC BEAD

Step 1: Cut the tube to your desired size. Using a yard of doubled thread, knot the end and sew into the plastic tube from inside to outside. Exit on the side about one-third up from the bottom (Figure 1).

Figure 1

Step 2: Ladder stitch around the tube. Make a stacked ladder by stringing an amount of beads all the same size to fit around your tube, and passing through all again. Pass through the first five just strung. *String 5 beads and pass through the previous five and the five just strung. Repeat from * to create a stacked ladder (Figure 2). When the ladder is long enough to circle the tube, pass through the first and last stack of beads added in this step to make a

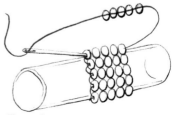

Figure 2

ring. Sew into the tube and back into the beadwork a couple of times to prevent your beads from slipping. Be careful when you sew through the tube—needles break easily during this step. Use a pair of pliers to gently pull the needle through so it doesn't bend. Do not sew straight across the middle of the tube or you might clog the hole of your bead. Exit the tube close to the spot where you entered it at one of the end stacked beads.

Step 3: String 8 of the same size beads. Begin brick stitch by passing under the next exposed loop between the ladder round made in Step 2 (Figure 3). Pull tight so the eight-bead strand folds in half. Pass through the last four strung. *String 4. Pass under the next exposed loop and back through the four just strung. Repeat from * all around the tube, adjusting the number and placement of stacks to compensate for the bead stacks from Step 2. For example, you may find that you pass under every other loop from the previous round if those beads are small, but you'll pass through loops more than once if those beads are big. Use your judgment as you go. Pass down through the first four cubes added in this step. Weave through the beads so you exit at the other end of the initial seed-bead stacks.

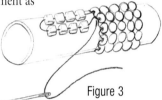

Figure 3

Step 4: Work brick stitch until the tube no longer shows. Weave through the beads to exit where you'd like to embellish.

EMBELLISHMENT IDEAS

• Make tiny fringe by stringing 1–2 beads. String 1 smaller bead. Pass back through the last beads strung and back into the basic bead. Weave to the next space over and repeat until you have little spikes sticking out all the way around.

• String a strand of beads that will fit around the basic bead. Pass through the first bead strung. Pull tight and tack the beads down to the basic bead. For a variation on this theme, make two rounds next to each other and one on top in the center.

• Exit from a large bead. String a bugle or an even number of seed beads or Delicas, using a different shape or color bead for the center. String a bugle or repeat the seed bead combination and stitch into the next large bead on your basic bead. Make sure the length of the bead combination is longer than the space you are bridging; the beads will stick out a bit to give you another dimension.

• Create a spiral by stringing beads diagonally across the belly of the bead or even along the entire length.

Jeannette Cook has been creating wonderful beaded art and art to wear for thirty-four years and teaching workshops for seventeen years. She teaches nationally and is co-owner of Beady-Eyed Women® with Vicki Star. The two are credited with eight books between them. Contact Jeannette at bdidwmn@aol.com; www.beadyeyedwomen.com; (619) 469-0254.

Netted Ovals

Liz Ofstead

This very versatile bead can be used alone or connected to others using tubular peyote to make a stunning piece of jewelry. Contrast your base bead color with the seed beads for maximum visual effect.

Materials
9/16" x 1" oval base bead
Size 11° seed beads in two colors, A and B
Size B beading thread in color to match oval base bead

Notions
Size 12 beading needle
Scissors
Beeswax

Round 1: Using 1½ yards of doubled waxed thread and leaving a 4" tail, string 5 A and tie into a circle.

Round 2: *String 1 A. Pass through the next bead on the circle. Repeat from * around to add five beads total. Exit from the first bead added in this round.

Round 3: *String 1 B. Pass through the next bead from the previous round. Repeat from * around to add five beads total. Exit from the first bead added in this round.

Round 4: String 1 A, 1 B, 1 A. Pass through the next bead from the previous round. Repeat from * around. Exit through the first two beads added in this round.

Round 5: Repeat Round 4.

Round 6: *String 2 A, 1 B, 2 A. Pass through the middle bead of the next net from the previous round. Repeat from * around. Exit through the first three beads added in this round.

Round 7: Repeat Round 6.

Round 8: String 3 A, 1 B, 3 A. Pass through the middle bead of the next net from the previous round. Repeat from * around. Exit through the first four beads added in this round.

Round 9: Repeat Round 8.

Round 10: Repeat Round 6 and insert the base bead into the netted tube.

Round 11: Repeat Round 6.

Round 12: Repeat Round 4.

Round 13: Repeat Round 4.

Round 14: *String 1 A and pass through the middle bead of the next net from the previous round. Repeat from * around to add five beads total. Exit from the first bead added in this round.

Round 15: *String 1 A and pass through the next bead from the previous round. Repeat from * around to add five beads total. Weave through several beads to secure. Tie a knot between threads, pass through more beads to hide the knot, and trim the thread close to the work. Weave in and trim the tail.

It's simple to connect the beaded beads with a peyote tube. Do so by working tubular peyote off the ends of the bead at Round 2 and/or Round 14.

Liz Ofstead is a psychologist and artist who loves to work in a variety of media. She especially enjoys beading with friends who form the Beadheads started by her mentor and friend, Diane Fitzgerald.

Beaded Beaded Beads

Nikia Angel

Warning: These beads are addictive. As you make more and more, you will learn that they become studies in texture, form, and color. The possibilities are endless!

You can find your core beads at any hobby shop, but don't just look in the bead section. There are plenty of wooden shapes in places like the dollhouse section, too.

Materials
Large-holed round or oval 12mm wooden bead
Size 6°, 11°, and 14° seed beads
Delicas
3mm–4mm round fire-polished beads
3mm–4mm round crystal beads
2mm–4mm fringe and accent beads (drops, druks, triangles, cubes, flowers, Tiny Tims)
Size B beading thread

Notions
Size 12 beading needle
Scissors
Beeswax
Pliers

BASIC BEAD

Step 1: Using 2 yards of waxed thread, string enough size 11's to wrap around the circumference of your bead. Make sure the number of beads is even and preferably divisible by 3 or 4. Pass through all the beads to form a ring. Keep the beads tight and tie a square knot.

Step 2: Work peyote stitch around the ring you just made. Fit the ring onto your bead to make sure that it fits snugly. Work another round and put the ring on the wooden bead.

Step 3: Work peyote stitch around the circumference of the bead. If the ring slips off the bead, pass through the hole of the core bead and back to the peyote-stitched ring. Weave through the ring and exit from the place you left off (Figure 1).

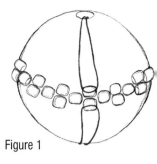

Figure 1

Continue working until the beadwork slightly sticks out from the bead. At this point begin making decreases. Do so by working regular peyote stitch and at determined points simply pass through a space instead of stringing a bead (Figure 2). Pull tight. In the next round add one bead over the decrease and continue working as normal. Another way of decreasing is to add a smaller bead between two size 11's and decrease gradually so that you end up using all small beads.

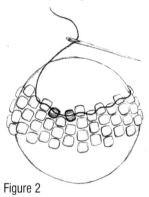

Figure 2

The best way to determine your decrease points is to divide your initial bead count at the circumference by thre Figure 2 Use this result to space your decreases in the round. For example, twenty-four circumference beads divided by four equals six. That means you should make a decrease every six beads.

Step 4: Continue decreasing as necessary, keeping a tight tension. When you get to the hole, pass through the last round and pull tight. Pass through the core bead's hole and into one of the beads on the other side of the peyote work. Repeat Steps 2–4 to complete the other side of the bead. Weave through the beads so that you exit from a bead at the circumference.

EMBELLISHMENT IDEAS

Embellishing beaded beads can be tricky over such tight bead-work. A size 12 or 13 needle works well. Also use a pliers to ease your needle through tough spots. There is a myriad of embellishment options. Here are two I like.

• String an accent bead and pass through the bead directly in line (not diagonal) with your bead. Continue all around to achieve a Saturn-like look (Figure 3).

Figure 3

• Make a three-bead picot by stringing three beads and pass-ing through the bead directly in line with your beads. Con-tinue around for a ruffled look.

Nikia Angel has been beading obsessively for over fifteen years. When not in her bead room surrounded by beads she is at work man-aging a bead store in Albuquerque and trying to "hook" new beaders.

Turquoise Elegance

Janie Warnick

You won't believe how sensuous this bead is until you make one of your own.

Materials
Delica beads
Size 8° seed beads
Size 15° seed beads
African turquoise chips
3mm cubes
Size O or D beading thread

Notions
Size 12 beading needle
Knitting needle or toothpick
Lighter or glue

BASE BEAD

Step 1: Using 3' of doubled thread, string a tension bead. String 12 Delicas. Pass through the first, third, fifth, seventh, ninth, eleventh, and twelfth beads. Pull very tight to create the first two rounds of a peyote tube. Work tubular peyote using size 8° for ten rounds, stepping up at the end of each round.

Step 2: Work two rounds using Delicas. Pass through the last round again and pull tight to make the opening as small as possible. Tie a surgeon's knot and trim. Finish by burning or placing a drop of glue on the knot.

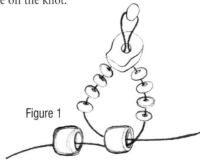

Figure 1

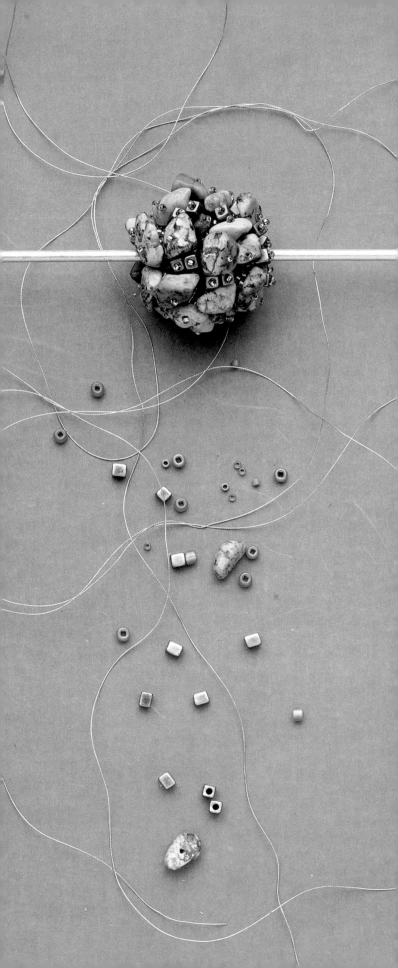

EMBELLISHING

Using 3' of single thread, weave through several of the base beads to anchor the thread on the first size 8° round. Begin a fringe by *passing through one of the size 8°s. String 4 size 15°s, 1 chip, and 1 size 15°. Pass back through the chip. String 4 size 15°s and pass through the other side of the size 8° you just exited. Pull tight. Move up to the next round and pass through the nearest size 8°.

String 4 size 15°s, 1 cube, and 1 size 15°. Pass back through the cube. String 4 size 15°s. Pass through the other side of the size 8 you just exited. Move back to the chip round and pass through the next size 8°. Repeat from * all around. When you have completed the round, move to the size 8° in the next base round. Work the same fringed embellishment as described above using 5 size 15°s, 1 chip, and 1 cube. Continue making fringe on each round of beads, increasing to 6 size 15°s on the third round. On subsequent rounds, work in reverse. Weave your thread through several beads to secure. Tie a knot and trim close to the work.

Yesterday, Janie Warnick sewed, embroidered, and quilted. Today, she beads.

Flowers and Vines

Jeri Herrera

A springtime flavor is what you'll taste with this bead.

Materials
Navy, white, light blue, grass green, yellow, red, pink, purple, and orange Delicas
Assorted flower-colored Delicas
20mm wooden bead
Cobalt blue paint
Varnish (optional)
Size B white and yellow beading thread
Fray Check

Notions
Size 12 needle
Scissors
Paint brush

Step 1: Paint the wooden bead blue, let dry, varnish if desired, and set aside.

Step 2: Work circular peyote.

Round 1: Using 3' of white thread and leaving a 4" tail, string 12 white. Tie the ends together with a square knot, leaving a 4" tail. Apply a small amount of Fray Check to the knot.

Round 2: *Pass through two white from Round 1. String 1 light blue and pass through the next two white. Repeat from * around to add 6 total.

Round 3: Using light blue, *string 2 and pass through 1 from Round 2. Repeat from * all round the circle.

Round 4: Using navy, *string 1 and pass through 1 from Round 3. Repeat from * all around the circle.

Round 5: Repeat Round 4.

Round 6: Pass through 1 from Round 5 and string 2 navy. Pass through 4 from Round 5 and string 1 light blue. Repeat from * all around the circle to add 6 total (Figure 1).

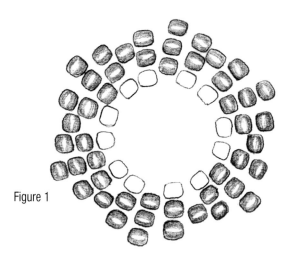

Figure 1

Repeat Rounds 1–6 to make a second circle.

Step 3: Create six odd-count peyote strips 27 rows long and three beads wide. Use navy for the edge beads and alternate light blue and white for the middle beads (Figure 2).

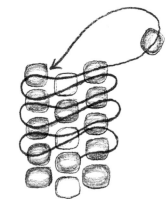

Figure 2

Step 4: Anchor 1' of thread to one of the circles created in Step 2. Repeat with the second circle. *Sew one strip to one of the light blue beads protruding from circle. Sew the other end of the strip to a bead protruding from the second circle.

Repeat from * for four strips. Be sure to line up the circles properly. Insert the wooden bead between the circles. Attach the last 2 strips with the wooden bead in place.

Step 5: Using 3' of yellow thread and leaving a 4" tail, string several green beads and pass over and under the strips so the green beads lay loosely around the wooden bead. This is the bead's vine. Tie a knot with the tail.

Pass through the first few green strung. String 10–12 green, skip 3–4 beads on the vine and pass through a few more beads to create leaves.

Step 6: Create flowers by passing through green beads and exiting from the vine or a leaf. String 1 yellow and 1 red. Pass through the yellow. *String 1 red. Pass through the yellow. Repeat from * placing 6 red beads around the yellow bead. String 1 yellow and pass back down through the first yellow added. Apply a drop of Fray Check and let dry. Pass through vine beads and exit at the next place you'd like to add a flower and repeat this step.

Make flowers all around the wooden bead for a garden effect. When you are through adding flowers tie a knot between beads, pass through more beads, and trim the thread close to the work.

Jeri Herrera has been beading for the last nine years and teaches in her local community. Jeri can be reached at jeri@dbeadmama.com or www.dbeadmama.com.

Spirals

Sandy Amazeen

This wild bead was inspired by the popular Dutch spiral beaded ropes. Add to the excitement of the bead by incorporating a variety of drops, tiny daggers, and other oddly shaped beads in a range of colors. Experimenting with bead and round counts will also give you surprising results. Be sure to keep your thread tension tight and even to achieve the best shape.

Materials
Size 11° seed beads in 5 colors (A, B, C, D, E)
Size 8° hex beads
3mm accent beads
4mm accent beads
Drop beads
Power Pro 30# test thread

Notions
Size 12 beading needles
Scissors

Round 1: Using a 4' length of thread and leaving a 4" tail, string 4 A, and tie into a circle. Pass through the first bead strung.

Round 2: *String 1 A and pass through the next bead on the circle. String 1 B and 1 C. Pass through the next bead on the circle. Repeat from * twice to add six beads total. Exit from the first bead added in this round.

Rounds 3–8: Work the rounds in tubular peyote stitch with no increases. Always string the same color bead that you have exited. After you have completed these rounds, thread a needle onto the tail thread, weave it into the beadwork, and trim close to the work.

Round 9: Using the working thread, string 3 size 11's and pass through the next bead of the previous round. Continue around in single-drop peyote stitch, always adding the same color bead that you have exited. End the round by passing through the first bead added in this round.

Round 10: String 1 size 11°, one 3mm, 1 size 11° and pass through the next bead of the previous round. Continue around in one-drop peyote stitch.

Round 11: String 2 size 11°s, one 3mm, 1 size 11°, 1 hex, 2 size 11°s and pass through the next bead of the previous round. Continue around in one-drop peyote stitch.

Round 12: String 2 size 11°s, one 3mm, 1 size 11°, 1 hex, 1 size 11°, one 4mm, 1 size 11° and pass through the next bead of the previous round. Continue around in one-drop peyote stitch.

Round 13: String 2 size 11°s, one 3mm, 1 size 11°, 1 hex, 1 size 11°, one 4mm, 1 size 11°, 1 drop, 2 size 11°s and pass through the next bead of the previous round. Continue around in one-drop peyote stitch.

Rounds 14–29: Repeat Round 13.

Rounds 30–42: Work Rounds 13–2, reversing the order so the spiral tapers down.

Round 43: *String 1 size 11° and pass through the next bead of the previous round. Repeat from * to add 4 beads total.

Weave through several beads and tie a knot between beads. Pass through more beads to hide the knot and trim the thread close to the work.

Sandy Amazeen is a frustrated painter who taught herself weaving, spinning, knitting, stained glass, and jewelry making while traveling the continent. What refuses to come out of her head to appear on canvas is coaxed to life through a number of other outlets including beadwork, which she has enjoyed for thirty years.

Four Square

Sharon Bateman

Make a few layers of this simple square bead to create a sensationally simple spacer. Or make more layers and spike them with fringe or loops to make a fuzzy ball of beads.

Materials
2–3 colors of seed beads in all the same size
Size B or D beading thread in color to match the beads

Notions
Size 12 beading needle
Scissors

Step 1: Using 3' of thread and leaving a 2" tail, string 8 beads and tie a knot. Trim the tail.

Step 2: Square stitch 2 beads onto 2 beads around the circle (Figure 1). Close the round by running through the first set of 2 beads. Begin a new round by stringing 2
beads and square-stitching to the set you just exited. Make a small spacer with two rounds. Make a larger spacer by adding rounds until you reach the desired length.

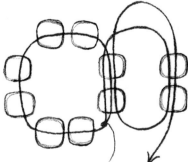

Figure 1

Step 3: Once you have completed the last round, turn the bead into a square shape by stringing a bead onto each corner of each round. Begin by *stringing 1 bead. Pass through the next 2 beads. Repeat three times to add four beads total (Figure 2). Pull tight and pass through the first set of 2 beads in the next round. Repeat from *, working in the opposite direction. Manipulate the beads to square off the round. When all the rounds are squared make a knot between beads and trim close to the work.

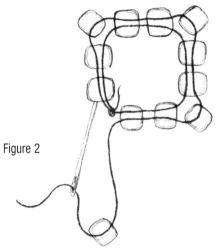

Figure 2

VARIATIONS

• Create tapered ends by working each end round with 4 beads instead of 8. Do so by stringing 4 beads and tying them into a circle. Square stitch 2 beads onto each of the 4 beads. Work the number of rounds desired for length. Taper the end by working 1 bead onto each of the sets of 2. Finish by squaring off the rounds.

• Make a bead cap by stringing 4 beads and tying them into a circle. Square stitch a second round of 4 beads. Square stitch 2 beads to 2 beads for two more rounds. Finish by squaring off the rounds.

• Fashion a fringe bead by making a base bead of any length and working basic fringe off of each bead on the base.

Sharon Bateman lives in northern Idaho and has been beading professionally since the early 1990s. She can be reached for questions or comments at www.sharonbateman.com.

Warped Jack

Sharon Bateman

This clever warp and weft technique helps to easily achieve perfection while covering a base bead with seed beads. Try your hand with this simple pumpkin, and then do your own thing!

Materials
1 oval 25 x 20 wooden bead
1 hank of orange 15° charlottes
1 strand of black 15° charlottes
Size O off-white or gray beading thread

Notions
Round file
Size 15 beading needle
Scissors
Permanent marker

Step 1: Draw a jack-o-lantern face on your wooden bead. If the hole in your bead is rough, you can use a round file to smooth the edges.

Step 2: Using 3' of thread, pass through the wooden bead and tie the end around the bead. Make the thread snug and let the knot rest at the inside edge of the hole.

Step 3: Pass through the wooden bead's hole three times so that you have thread placed at the north, south, east, and west sides of the bead (Figure 1). These will serve as warp threads.

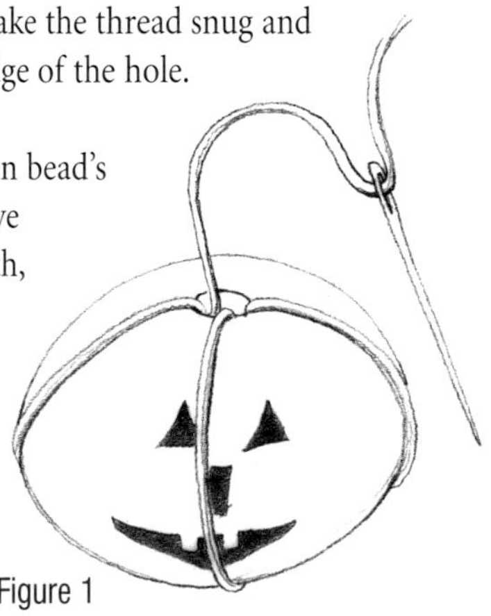

Step 4: Pass through the wooden bead's hole four more times, placing each wrapped thread between the warp threads placed in Step 3. Hold the tension on your thread at all times so you keep your threads snug.

Figure 1

Step 5: Pass under one of the warp threads. As you pull your thread tight, it will form a loop at the base of the thread. Pass your needle through the loop and pull tight to create a half-hitch knot (Figure 2). Work a half-hitch on each of the threads along the edge of the bead hole.

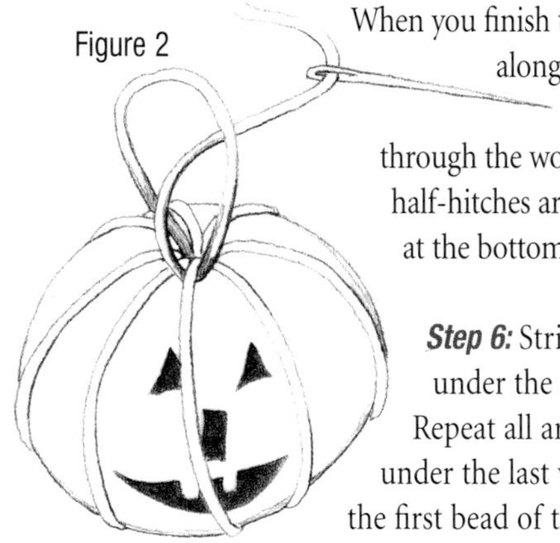

When you finish the half-hitches along the top of the bead, pass down through the wooden bead and make half-hitches around the threads at the bottom of the bead.

Figure 2

Step 6: String 1 orange. Pass under the next warp thread. Repeat all around (Figure 3). Pass under the last warp thread and through the first bead of the round. Pull snug and pass under the next warp thread.

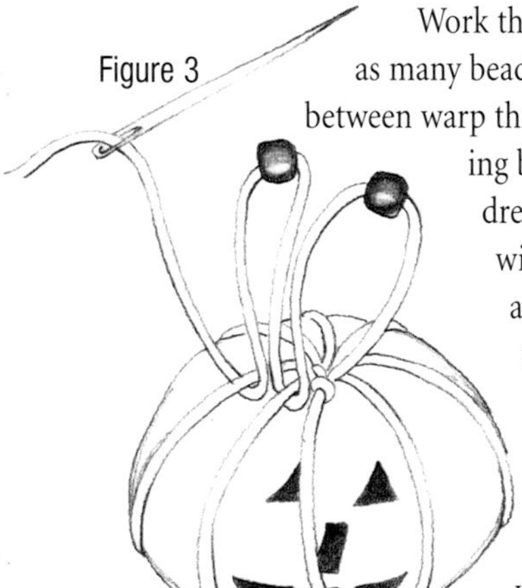

Work the consecutive rounds, adding as many beads as needed to fill the space between warp threads. Work the face by placing black beads over the face you drew in with the marker. There will most likely be some trial and error on the bead count in this step.

Figure 3

Step 7: Work the bead until you reach the opposite hole, completely covering your wooden bead. Secure your thread and trim close to work.

Sharon Bateman lives in northern Idaho and has been beading professionally since the early 1990s. She can be reached for questions or comments at www.sharonbateman.com.

Wirewovens

Bethany Barry

Instructions for these wonderful wirewoven beads have been kept secret until now. Enjoy making and wearing them—and maintain the mystery!

Materials
22-, 24-, or 26-gauge wire
Size 6°, 8°, and 11° seed beads
Assortment of small accent beads (magatamas, teardrops, triangles, daggers, leaves, flowers, hearts, round glass, Miracle beads, Bali silver beads, semiprecious stone chips, etc.)

Notions
Twist 'n Curl tool
Wire cutters
Round-nosed pliers
Chain-nosed pliers

Step 1: Use 3' of wire to wrap around the Twist 'n Curl tool. Read the manufacturer's directions to make a 3½" coil. Remove the coil and thread an 18" piece of the same-gauge wire through the center of the coil. Wrap one end of this wire 4–6 times around the tool at one end of the bead. This will be the beaded bead's end. Wrap the 3½" coil around the tool right next to the bead end to make a cylindrical 1½" bead. Use the other end of the loose wire to wrap around the tool 4–6 times at the other end of the cylindrical bead (Figure 1). Leave the cylindrical bead on the tool so the bead will hold its shape.

Figure 1

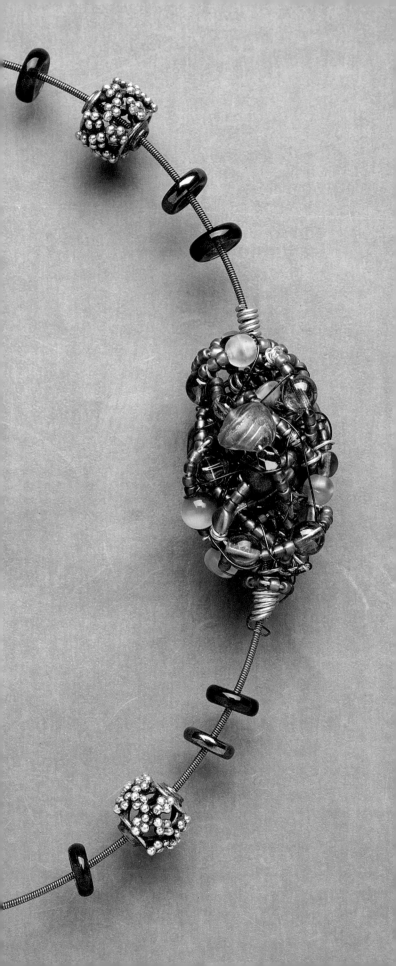

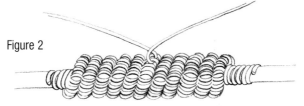

Figure 2

Step 2: Attach the center of a 3' wire to a coil loop in the middle of the cylindrical bead. This will be your weaving wire. Put one end to the side (Figure 2).

Step 3: Use the other end of the weaving wire to string a small section of size 8° or 11° seed beads. Loop the string of beads in and around another part of the cylinder bead, moving around the bead at an angle.

If there isn't enough space within a loop of the coil to hook the beaded wire through, use your pliers to gently open enough space. Continue to fill the weaving wire with seed beads and accent beads.

Work your way around the bead, making sure to fill it evenly. You are creating a foundation from which to work (Figure 3). After you've circumnavigated the base bead with one length of wire, leave a 1" space at the end of the wire and set aside.

Figure 3

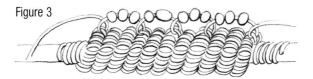

Step 4: Repeat Step 3 for the other end of the wire, weaving and crisscrossing the seed-bead-filled wires that are already there. You can also pass the wire through larger beads to anchor them or go under other wires. If the weaving wire breaks, wind it back into the beads and wire, hiding the end carefully so that it doesn't show and cut you or the wearer. Add a new wire by anchoring it around one of the coil loops and continue weaving. Be sure you cover every inch of the base cylindrical bead to hide the coil. Add more wire if necessary.

Step 5: When both ends of the weaving wire are filled and connected to the cylindrical bead, wrap the ends around other wires and pass through beads to hide. Trim the wire ends close to the bead.

Bethany Barry has been working and playing with beads for over twenty years. She lives in Vermont, teaches bead classes nationally, and is writing a book on bead crochet.

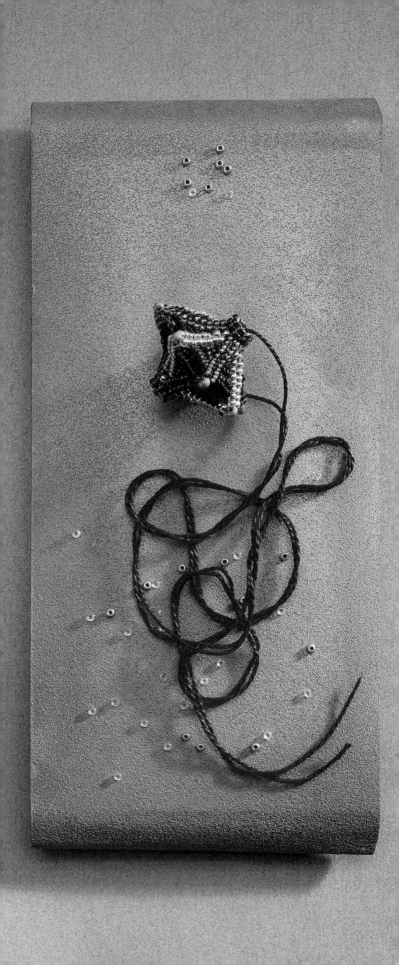

Pinwheels

Carole Horn

This crisp bead evokes the playfulness of a child's pinwheel or a Chinese lantern. Have fun with color choices as you make your own version.

Materials
Size 11° seed beads in three colors (A, B, C)
Size 15° seed beads (D)
Size D beading thread in color to complement beads

Notions
Size 12 beading needle
Scissors
Beeswax

Rounds 1 and 2: Using 3 yards of doubled thread and leaving a 4" tail, use A to make a stacked ladder 2 beads high and 8 beads long. Join the first and last 2 bead stacks to form a circle. Your tail and working threads should exit from the opposite ends of the same stack.

Round 3: Heavily wax your thread so it becomes sticky. Begin working herringbone stitch by stringing 2 A. Pass down through the top bead of the adjacent stack and up through the top bead of the next stack. Continue around until you have added 6 beads. String 2 A. Pass down through the top bead in the next stack and up through the top 2 beads in the following stack to make a step up. *Note:* Keeping your thread tight and heavily waxed will ensure the stability of this self-supporting bead.

Round 4: *String 2 A and pass down through the next bead. String 1 B and pass up through the next bead. Repeat from * around until you have 4 pairs of A with a B between the pairs. Step up by passing up through 2 A.

Round 5: *String 2 A and pass down through the next A. String 2 B and pass up through the first bead of the next A pair. Repeat from * until you have 4 pairs of A with 2 B between each pair. Step up.

Round 6: *String 2 A, pass down through the next A and up through the first B in the pair. String 2 B, pass down through the next B and up through the next A. Repeat from * around, adding 2 A over 2 A and 2 B over 2 B. Step up.

Step 7: *String 2 A and pass down through next A. String 1 D and pass up through the next B. String 2 B and pass down through the next B. String 1 D and pass up through the next A. Repeat from * all around and step up.

Steps 8–11: Repeat Step 7 but increase 1 D in each section for each succeeding round. Step 11 should have 8 spokes with 5 D between each of them. Exit from the first bead of the nearest spoke.

Step 12: Add a single bead at the end of each spoke by *stringing 1 C and passing down through two spoke beads, the adjacent 5 D, and up through two beads of the next spoke. Repeat from * around to add * 8 C. Weave through several beads, tie a knot between beads, pass through more beads to hide the knot, and trim the thread close to the work.

FINISHING

Make a second herringbone disk by repeating Steps 1–11. Do not cut your thread.

*Pass through a C from the first disk. Pass down through the next bead on the second disk. Pass through the adjacent 5 D and up through the first bead of the next spoke. Repeat from * to attach the first and second disks.

Carole Horn is a native New Yorker who has taught beading classes for the past twelve years. She can be reached at (212) 682-7474.

Bead Cage

Barb Switzer

Never underestimate the beauty of hardware! This dazzling bead gives testimony to that feature.

Materials
½" hardware cloth
30-gauge Artistic wire
3mm–9mm beads
2 Bali silver 10mm bead caps
10mm–12mm findings that have loops
Hypo Tube cement

Notions
Safety glasses
Dremel tool with fiberglass cutter blades
Metal cutters (not jewelry wire cutters)
File
Chain-nose pliers
Flush cutter
Round-nose pliers

Step 1: Put on your safety glasses. Use the Dremel tool and fiberglass cutter blades to cut the hardware cloth into a piece 1 × 4 squares long. You may also cut with a wire cutter, but file the sharp ends after cutting.

Step 2: Hold the piece with the chain-nose pliers so the pliers cross the hardware cloth at the second cross wire (Figure 1). Use your thumb to push the first square away from you. If the resulting bend is curved, squeeze it with the very back of the chain-nose pliers' jaw to create a 90-degree angle. Repeat from * for the next 2 wires to make a box.

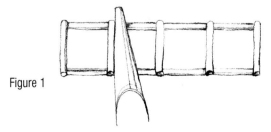

Figure 1

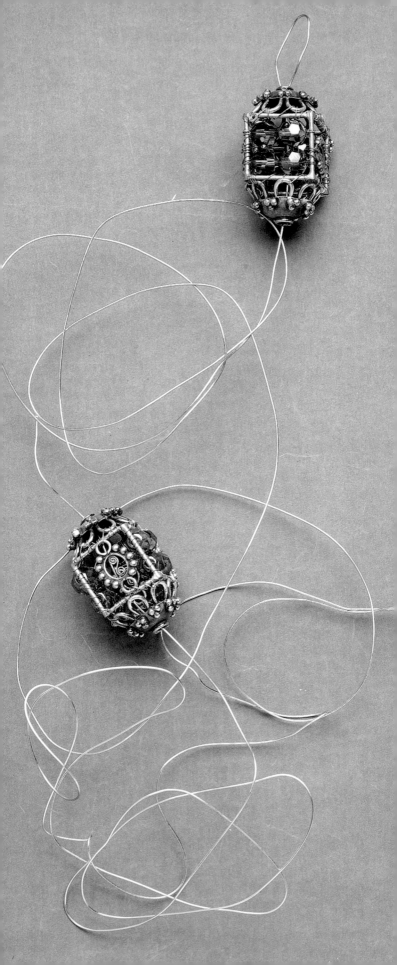

Step 3: Use the center of a 12"–18" length of wire to tie an overhand knot connecting the seam where the end bars of the hardware cloth come together. Make the connection about ⅓ of the way down the seam. Using one end of the wire, string enough beads to cross the square you are working in. Wrap the wire around the square's opposite bar and pull the wire tight. The beads should lie flat but a little wiggle room is good. Continue wrapping the wire on the same bar until you are positioned to add the next beads and go back across to the opposite and original bar (Figure 2). Keep wrapping around the box, filling all four sides with beads or findings. Try changing the orientation of the beads for an interesting look.

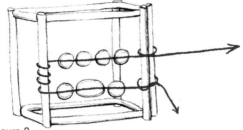

Figure 2

If you get into a tricky place with your wire, either wrap it around the frame or pass through the beads to reposition yourself. Once you're done with one half of the wire, use the other. To finish a wire, wrap the end around a bar five or six times and cut with a flush cutter, squeeze the end against the bar with a chain-nose pliers, and glue the end. Another way to end the wire is to make a tiny spiral, push it against the bar, and glue. If you run out of wire, begin a new piece as before.

It isn't necessary to wrap the seam closed. The box will keep its shape. But you can experiment by adding findings or beads across the seam for a bit of style.

Step 4: Once you have completed beading all four sides of the box, use 20-gauge wire to attach one bead cap to each end of the beaded bead. Do so like you have attached the other elements of the cage, wrapping the loops of the cap to the bars of the hardware cloth.

Barb Switzer is a beadwork teacher, engineer, jeweler, and graphic designer. She thanks the Fusion Betties for great ideas, big laughs, Sunday night TV, irreplaceable artistic inspiration, and for convincing her these beads are weird but cool.

Melon Bead

Sharri Moroshok

Use your regular-sized seed beads for this project, but sort out your thick and thin ones to help make clean increases and decreases. The more smooth the beaded surface, the more precise the geometric design of this lovely little bead.

Materials
12mm round wooden bead
Size 13° charlottes (A)
Size 14° seed beads in three contrasting colors (B, C, D)
Size B beading thread in color to complement beads

Notions
Size 13 beading needles
Scissors

Step 1: Using 2 yards of thread and leaving a 1" tail, string 1 thick C. Tie an overhand knot. Using all thick beads *string A, B, A, C, D, B, A, C, A, B, D. Repeat from * three times to string a total of 48.

Pass through the first few beads just strung to make a tight circle. Hold the circle closed and slide it around the circumference of the wooden bead so it fits snugly. If the circle is too loose or too tight, restring and adjust the width of the beads as needed. When the fit is right, remove the circle from the base bead. Pass through all the beads once more, ending with the first bead strung.

Step 2, Round 1: Work single-drop peyote stitch in the round using an A, A, D sequence. Repeat seven times. Exit from the first A.

Round 2: Work B, C, B, C. Repeat five times. Exit from the first B.
Round 3: Using thinner beads, work A, D, A, A, D, A. Repeat three times. Exit from the first A. Making sure the tail lies underneath, gently slide the beadwork onto the circumference of the wooden bead.

Round 4: Work C, B, C, B, C, decrease 1 (make a decrease by passing through the next bead without adding a bead). Repeat three times. Exit from the first C.

Round 5: Work D, A, A, D, 2 A (2 beads worked in the space between beads). Repeat three times. Exit from the first D.

Round 6: Work B, C, B, C, pass through both As of the previous round, C. Repeat three times. Exit from the first B.

Step 3: Weave through the beads diagonally so that you exit from the other side of the beginning of the beadwork, at the first A of a stripe that was decreased on the first side. Adjust the beadwork as necessary so that the first round is at the center of the wooden bead.

Round 1: Work B, C, B, C. Repeat five times. Exit from the first B.

Round 2: Work A, D, A, A, D, A. Repeat three times. Exit from the first A.

Round 3: Work C, B, C, B, C, decrease 1. Repeat three times. Exit from the first C.

Round 4: Work D, A, A, D, 2 A. Repeat 3 times. Exit from the first D.

Round 5: Work B, C, B, C, pass through both As of the previous round, C. Repeat three times. Exit from the first B. Center your work on the base bead.

Round 6: Work A, A, D, thick C, D. Repeat three times. Exit from the first A.

Round 7: Decrease 1, B, C, C, B. Repeat three times. Exit from the first B.

Round 8: Work D, decrease 1, D, 2 As. Repeat three times. Exit from the first D.

Round 9: Work a thick C, B, B. Repeat three times. Exit from the first C.

Round 10: Work D, a thick B, D. Repeat three times. Exit from the first D.

Round 11: Work B, B, D. Repeat three times. Exit from the first B.

Round 12: Decrease 1, D, D. Repeat three times. Pass through the next 2 Bs and the next 3 Ds.

Round 13: Work B, decrease 1. Repeat three times. Reinforce the round by weaving through the beads two or three times. Weave the thread through several more beads in subsequent rounds to secure; trim close to the work.

Step 4: Begin a new thread and exit from a B that lies before a long C stripe section. Repeat Step 3, Rounds 6–13 to complete this side.

Sharri Moroshok's passion for beaded beads began in 1994 when she made her first attempts to cover a plain wooden bead with lovely seed beads. The meditative quality and joy of the process have captivated her ever since. See more of her work at www.BeadedBeads.com.

Star Flower

Diane Fitzgerald

This glistening star is created with triangle stitch. Make a variety of flowers by using rice, bi-cone, round or oval fire-polished, or faceted beads.

Materials
3mm round faceted beads
Size 11° seed beads or Delicas
Size 8° seed beads
Size D beading thread

Notions
Size 10 beading needle
Scissors

Step 1: Using 2' of thread and leaving a 4" tail, string three 3mm and tie into a circle. Holding the beads with the knot at the bottom, pass back through the last bead strung.

Step 2: String two 3mms. Pass through the third bead strung in the previous step and the two beads just strung (beads 4 and 5) (Figure 1).

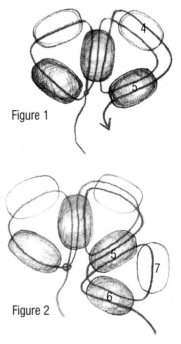

Figure 1

Step 3: String two 3mms (beads 6 and 7). Pass through beads 5 and 6 (Figure 2).

Step 4: String two 3mms (beads 8 and 9) Pass through beads 6, 8, and 9.

Step 5: String two 3mms (beads 10 and 11). Pass through beads 9 and 10.

Figure 2

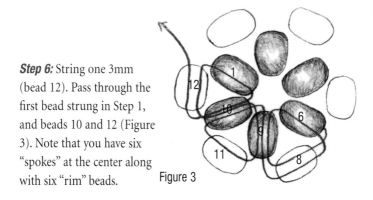

Step 6: String one 3mm (bead 12). Pass through the first bead strung in Step 1, and beads 10 and 12 (Figure 3). Note that you have six "spokes" at the center along with six "rim" beads.

Figure 3

Step 7: String two 3mms (beads 13 and 14). Pass through beads 12 and 13. Fold the beads just strung toward the center so they lie on top of the previous layer.

Step 8: String one 3mm (bead 15). Pass through beads 2, 13, and 15 and 4 (Figure 4).

Step 9: String one 3mm (bead 16). Pass through beads 15, 4, and 16.

Figure 4

Step 10: String bead 17. Pass through beads 7, 16, and 17.

Step 11: Pass through bead 8 and string bead 18. Pass through beads 17 and 8. Complete and strengthen the flower by passing through beads 18, 14, and 11, twice (Figure 5).

Step 12: *String 1 size 11° and pass through the next rim bead. Repeat from * all around to add 6 beads total.

Step 13: Pass down through the closest spoke bead. String 1 size 8° and pass through the opposite spoke bead. Turn the Star Flower bead over and add a second size 8° in the center. Weave through several beads, tie a knot between beads, pass through more to hide the knot, and trim the thread close to the work. Work in the tail thread.

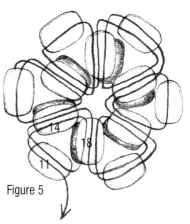

Figure 5

Like many of us, Diane Fitzgerald is addicted to beads. You may reach her at dmfbeads@bitstream.net.

Diamond Band

Linda Richmond

This bead is created in three steps: First you use the green iris
and gold Delicas to make a base bead of tubular peyote. Next
you add the crystal ends to the base bead. Finally you make
the diamond band that goes around the center of the base
bead, slide it on, and attach it.

Materials
Gold, green iris, and tourmaline Delica beads
4mm light amethyst satin and jonquil satin
   bicone crystals
Size 11° lime green seed beads
Lime green fringe drop beads
Size 0 and B thread to complement beads

Notions
Size 12 and 13 or 15 beading needles
Scissors
Beeswax

Step 1: Using 3' of size B doubled and well-waxed thread and
a size 12 needle, string 1 green and 1 gold leaving a 4" tail.
Repeat until you have 24 beads. Pass through the first bead
and hold onto the tail until you've completed the third round.

Step 2: Work 18 rounds of tubular peyote stitch using green.
Work an extra round using gold for a total of 21 rounds. Exit
from one of the end gold beads. This is your base bead.

Step 3: String 1 tourmaline, 1 amethyst crystal, and 1 tourmaline. Pass back through the crystal and string 1 tourmaline.
Skipping 1 gold on the base bead, pass through
the next one (Figure 1). Continue around,
alternating amethyst satin and jonquil
crystals. Exit from the tourmaline that
sits above the first crystal added in
this round.

Figure 1

Step 4: String 1 lime green seed bead and pass through the tourmaline that sits on top of the next crystal. Continue around to join all of the tourmalines. Pass through several beads, tie half-hitch knots between the beads, and pass though a few more and trim your thread close to the work. Weave your thread to the other end of the base bead, exiting from a gold bead, or start a new thread at the other end.

Step 5: Repeat Steps 3 and 4.

Step 6: Using 2' of size 0 thread, doubled and waxed, and a size 13 needle, string 7 tourmalines and 1 drop, leaving a 4" tail. Repeat until you've added 4 drops. Tie into a circle and pass through the first drop.

Step 7: Work a base round of tubular peyote stitch, incorporating the drops as you would the tourmalines.

Step 8: Work peyote stitch decreases between each drop to create one side of a diamond. Use a drop for the diamond's point (Figure 2). Work the diamonds in the round, not

Figure 2

individually. Weave through the beads back to your base round and repeat this step to create the other half of the diamond shapes. Do not cut your thread.

Step 9: Slide the diamond band over the base bead and center it. Secure your thread in the base bead and attach the band at each of the drops. Do this by passing through the beads under the drops so the thread is hidden. Weave your thread through the beads of the base bead to get from one drop to another.

After you have completely attached the band, zigzag through the beads to secure the thread and trim it close to the work.

Linda Richmond lives in Sandpoint, Idaho, and has been captivated by beads for most of her life. She launched a full-time beading career in 1995. She now sells her kits, along with beads, tools, books, and supplies, through her website at www.lindarichmond.com.

Story Beadz

Dona Anderson-Swiderek

Story Beadz tell a personal story. They tell what you feel, what you wanted to be when you grew up, or what you are now. They can also pay tribute to someone else—a mother, sister, grandmother, aunt, or friend. Make a prom queen, a cowgirl, or Batgirl! Just stretch your creativity and make it happen.

Materials

20mm wooden bead

Size 14° or 15° peach, dark peach, pink, white, blue, red, and black seed beads

Size 8°, 10°, 11°, and 14° gold, red, brown, black, or gray seed beads

Size 11° seed beads in accent colors

Size B beading thread in color to complement beads

Notions

Size 12 needles

Scissors

Step 1: Using 3' of thread and leaving a 4" tail, string beads following the chart to set up for tubular peyote. After completing the charted beads for Rounds 1 and 2, string 41–44 flesh beads, depending how many fit best around the base bead. Tie three tight knots and slip the circle over the base bead so it is very snug.

Pass through the first bead strung. Pass down through the base bead and through the first six beads of the circle. Pass down through the base bead and through the seventh through twelfth beads. Continue around, anchoring the beaded circle to the base bead at every sixth bead (Figure 1).

Figure 1

Step 2: Work the chart in tubular peyote. Once the beads begin no longer to lie flat on the base bead, work gradual decreases. Try to work the decreases at the sides and back of the head because those areas will be covered with embellishments. A decrease between the eyebrows is also a good choice. Always end and begin threads at the back of the head. Once you have covered the top half of the bead, work the bottom half.

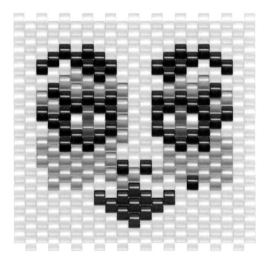

Step 3: Embellish your face bead in any way you wish.

To make a neck and work a collar, stop making decreases near the bottom of the bead and work a peyote tube. Create a netted or peyote ruffle collar.

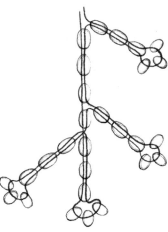

Branch fringe

Create "accessories." String beads to make a necklace which you sew around the neck. Make glasses by bending 30-gauge wire into the desired shape and sewing them to the sides of the head.

Always begin the hair at the bottom of the head and work ear to ear. Try branch, curly, or twisted fringe, or use a three-bead whip stitch. Mix bead sizes and textures.

Zigzag fringe

Try your hand at sculptural peyote and make a hat. Creating a circular peyote form and sewing it to a short piece of tubular peyote is one of the easiest techniques.

A regular contributor to Beadwork, *Dona Anderson-Swiderek is the author of the self-published books* Beading Heart Designs: Amulet Purses *and* Let's Face It. *Find Dona's teaching schedule on her website, http://members.tripod.com/~beadingheart.*

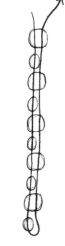

Curling Fringe

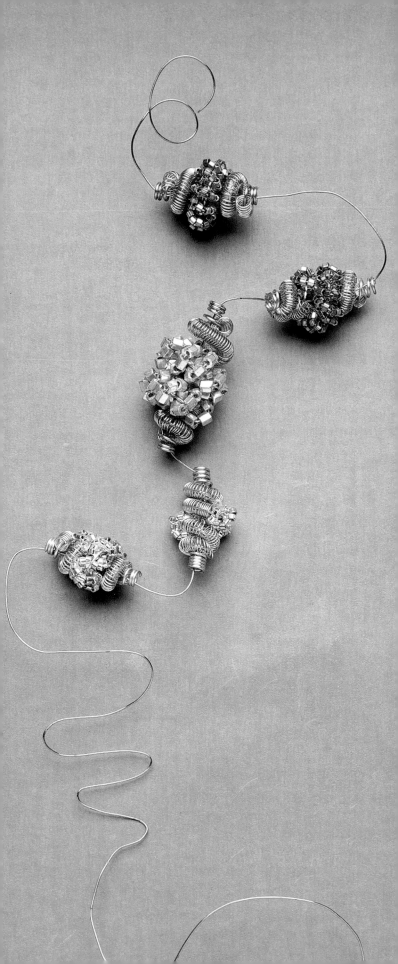

Delica/Wire Connection

Sheilah Cleary

These beautiful beads need only a coiling tool, wire, and Delicas to create. Whether you use them as spacer beads or on their own, you'll be glad you learned how to make them.

Materials
20-gauge non-tarnish gold wire
22-gauge non-tarnish gold wire
28-gauge non-tarnish gold wire
Gold Delica beads
Size B beading thread in color to match beads
E-6000 glue

Notions
Wire Worker® or other coiling tool
Wire cutter
Round-nose pliers
Needle-nose pliers
Toothpicks
Beading needle
Small sharp scissors

Step 1: Use the 28-gauge wire to string 6" of beads. Use the coiling tool's smallest mandrel to coil 1" of unbeaded wire. Keep the wire wrapped tight and the coils close together. Wrap the beaded wire, keeping the wire tight so no space is created between the beads. Coil another inch of unbeaded wire (Figure 1) and remove the coil from the mandrel. Trim the bead neatly so that no sharp wire ends protrude.

Figure 1

Step 2: Slide the coil you've just made onto a piece of 22-gauge wire and attach that wire to the coiling tool (Figure 2). Make a ½" coil. Carefully wrap the coil created in Step 1 around the mandrel, keeping the twists close together. Use the other end of the bare 22-gauge wire to make a ½" coil (Figure 3). Remove the coil from the mandrel and trim the plain wire coil to ³⁄₁₆" to complete the wire bead.

Figure 2

Figure 3

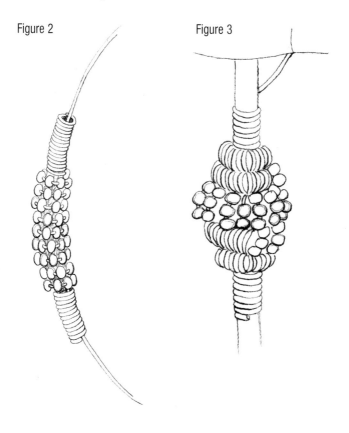

An international tutor and bead artist, Sheilah Cleary has been a crafter all her life. She can be reached at shebeads@aol.com for a schedule of upcoming classes, or go to www.shebeads.com.

Crystal Cluster

Doris Coghill

Inspired by the beautiful bead clusters she has seen on vintage jewelry, Doris has recreated the technique and shares it with us here. Stacked rings of beads are the secret, and combining them in different ways will give you a look all your own.

Materials
3 x 5 Czech cut crystal rondelles
26-gauge wire in a color to match the beads
Eye pins

Notions
Wire cutter
Round-nose pliers
Needle-nose pliers

Step 1: Cut 3" of wire. String an odd number of crystals and form a circle. Firmly twist the ends of the wire together. Allow the crystals to touch, but don't make it so tight that the crystals break. Trim the twisted wire about ¼" from the crystals. Use the needle-nose pliers to bend the wire to the inside of the circle (Figure 1).

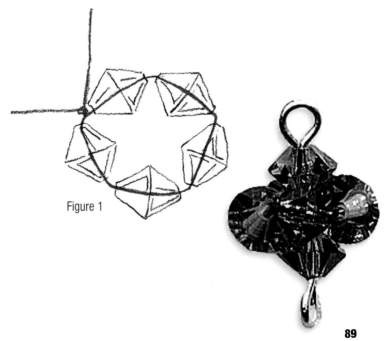

Figure 1

Step 2: String 1 crystal, ring(s) of crystals, and 1 crystal on an eye pin. Bend the end of the eye pin at a 45-degree angle right at the end crystal to keep everything snug. If more than one ring of crystals is used they should sit snugly together with the edges of one ring fitting into the spaces between the crystals in the ring above or below to it. Trim the pin about ¼" from the last crystal. Use the round-nose pliers to make a loop (Figure 2).

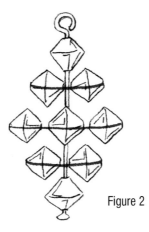

Figure 2

To make different sizes of clusters, follow these stringing sequences.

Small cluster: 1 crystal, one 5-crystal ring, 1 crystal.

Long cluster: 1 crystal, one 5-crystal ring, 1 crystal, one 7-crystal ring, 1 crystal, one 5-crystal ring, 1 crystal.

Large cluster: 1 crystal, one 5-crystal ring, one 9-crystal ring, 2 crystals, one 9-crystal ring, one 5-crystal ring, 1 crystal.

Doris Coghill has been working with seed beads for about nine years, but has been involved with some type of crafts all her life. She is currently busy with designing and teaching beadwork and working with her business, Dee's Place. She can be reached at www.beadsbydee.com.

Bead Royale

Jean Campbell

Wear this big bold bead on a simple chain or incorporate it into an elaborate necklace. Either way you'll look regal.

Materials
4 oval 11 × 9 Czech glass beads
16 bi-cone 6mm Austrian crystals
8 Bali silver flower spacers
Size 11° silver seed beads
Size D beading thread in color to complement beads

Notions
Beading needle
Scissors

Step 1: Use 1 yard of thread. Start ladder stitch by stringing 1 spacer, 1 size 11°, 1 crystal, 1 size 11°, 1 spacer, one 11 × 9, 1 spacer, 1 size 11°, 1 crystal, 1 size 11°, 1 spacer, one 11 × 9. Leaving a 3" tail, tie the beads in a tight circle with a square knot. Your knot will be at the bottom of the 11 × 9.

Step 2: Pass through the first spacer strung in the last step and continue passing through the next six beads, exiting from a spacer at the top of an 11 × 9. String 1 size 11°, 1 crystal, 1 size 11°, 1 spacer, one 11 × 9, 1 spacer, 1 size 11°, 1 crystal, and 1 size 11°. Pass up through the spacer at the bottom of the adjoining 11 × 9 (Figure 1). Pass up through the 11 × 9 and the spacer at the top. Pass through the size 11°, crystal, size 11°, 11 × 9, and spacer just strung.

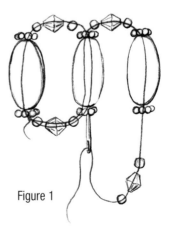

Figure 1

Step 3: String 1 size 11°, 1 crystal, 1 size 11°, 1 spacer, one 11 × 9, 1 spacer, 1 size 11°, 1 crystal, and 1 size 11°. Pass down through the spacer at the top of the 11 × 9 added in Step 2. Pass down through the 11 × 9 and the spacer at the bottom. Pass through the size 11°, crystal, size 11°, 11 × 9, and spacer just strung.

Step 4: String 1 size 11°, 1 crystal, and 1 size 11°. Pass down through the spacer at the top of the first 11 × 9 in the ladder (Figure 2). Pass down through the 11 × 9 and the spacer at the bottom. String 1 size 11°, 1 crystal, and 1 size 11°. Pass up through the spacer at the bottom of the first 11 × 9 in the ladder. Pass up through the 11 × 9 and the spacer at the top.

Figure 2

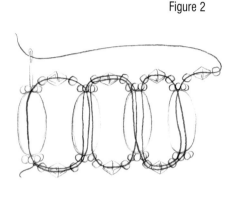

Step 5: *String 1 size 11°, 1 crystal, and 1 size 11°. Pass back through the crystal and size 11° to make a fringe leg. Pass through the next size 11°-crystal-size 11° sequence on the ladder. Repeat from * so that you have four fringe legs. Pass down through the closest spacer, 11 × 9, and spacer sequence on the ladder.

Step 6: Repeat Step 5 for the bottom of the bead.

Step 7: *Pass up through the fringe leg so you exit from the size 11° at the top. Pass through the size 11° at the top of the next fringe leg. Repeat from * so all the fringe legs are attached. Pull very tight and pass through all again. Pass down through a fringe leg, the closest spacer, 11 × 9, and spacer sequence on the ladder.

Step 8: Repeat Step 7 for the bottom of the bead.

Step 9: Weave through all beads again to strengthen and tighten the bead. Tie a knot between beads, pass through several more to hide the knot, and trim tails close to the bead.

Jean Campbell is the editor of Beadwork *magazine and books.*

Tartan

Sharon Bateman

This ingenious netted bead is wide open for bead size, color, and pattern experimentation. You'll first make a square-stitched base bead, work a series of nets over the core, and then intertwine a second set of nets through the first.

Materials
Size 11° seed beads in 2 colors (A and B)
Size B beading thread in color to complement beads

Notions
Size 12 beading needles
Scissors

BEADED CORE
Round 1: Using 3' of thread and leaving a 2" tail, string 10 beads, alternating A and B. Tie into a circle and trim the tail.

Round 2: *Square stitch 2 A onto the next 2 beads of the circle created in Round 1. Repeat from * all around the circle (Figure 1). Exit through the first two beads added in this round.

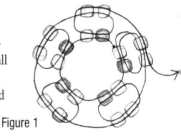

Figure 1

Rounds 3–9: Repeat Round 2 seven times so you have a tube nine rounds long.

Round 10: Repeat Round 2, but alternate beads A and B. Make sure the bead colors are in the same placement as in Round 1. Exit from an A.

FIRST NET
Round 1: *String 5 A and pass through the next A on the tube. Repeat from * around. Pass through the first 3 beads added in this round.

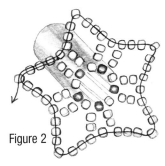

Round 2: *String 7 A. Pass through the middle bead of the next net. Repeat from * around. Pass through the first 4 beads added in this round (Figure 2).

Figure 2

Round 3: *String 9 A. Pass through the middle bead of the next net. Repeat from * around. Pass through the first 5 beads added in this round.

Rounds 4 and 5: Repeat Round 3.

Round 6: Repeat Round 2.

Round 7: *String 2 A. Pass through an A on the opposite end of the core bead. String 2 A and pass through the middle bead of the next net. Repeat from * around. Close the round by passing through the first 2 beads added in this round and the closest two beads on the core. Exit from a B.

SECOND NET

Round 1: *String 5 B and pass through the next B on the core. Pull tight. Repeat from * around. Pass through the first 3 beads added in this round.

Rounds 2–6: Using B, repeat Rounds 2–6 of the A net, but pass over and under the A net legs so the strands of A and B beads intertwine (Figure 3).

Figure 3

Round 7: String 2 B. Pass under the next A net and through a B core bead. *String 2 B and pass through the middle bead of the next B net. Repeat from * all around. Weave through several beads, tie a knot between beads, pass through more beads to hide the knot, and trim the thread close to the work.

Sharon Bateman lives in northern Idaho and has been beading professionally since the early 1990s. She can be reached for questions or comments at www.sharonbateman.com.

Carnival Tubes

Teresa Barrett

Using a varied combination of shapes and colors turns this beaded bead into a fanciful carnival!

Materials
1–1½" clear or semi-opaque drinking straw
Size 2 Japanese matte twisted bugles
Size 11° Japanese seed beads in two colors, A and B
Size 14° Japanese seed beads
Tiny drops
Silamide thread to match beads

Notions
Size 11 sharps needles
Scissors
Hypo Tube cement

BASIC BEAD

Step 1: Tie a large knot at the end of 1 yard of thread. Sew through the straw from the inside out, ⅛" from one end. Glue the knot to the straw.

Step 2: Working tight against the bottom of the straw, build a ladder of 12 bugles. Join the twelfth bugle to the first bugle to form a tube around the straw. Exit the working thread from the top of the bugle toward the top of the straw. Push the bugle tube down to the bottom edge of the straw. *Note:* Avoid using chipped or broken bugles—they will fray the thread and eventually cut it. If you still have trouble with the bugles cutting the thread, string a size 11° of the same color on each end of the bugles and treat the three of them as one bugle bead. When you are adding the embellishments to these units, keep the thread away from the edges of the bugles.

Step 3: String 1 A, 1 B, 2 A, 1 B, 1 A. Begin working in three-stacked brick stitch by passing from back to front through the first loop of thread between the bugles in the previous row. Pass back through the last three beads just strung. Continue around working brick stitch using 1 A, 1 B, and 1 A. Consider this three-bead unit as one. At the end of the round, pass down through the first beads added in this round, pass back to front through the last empty loop of the previous row, and pass back up through the first three beads added in the round.

Step 4: Work this round in brick stitch using bugles.

Step 5: Work this round in brick stitch using color A.

Step 6: Carefully cut the excess straw off at the top of the bead.

Step 7: String 3 size 14's and pass back to front through the next thread loop. Pass back through the last bead added. String 2 size 14's. Pass back to front through the next thread loop, and back through the last bead added. Continue around the bead. End by adding one bead and passing down through the first bead added in this round. Pass back to front through the last empty thread loop and pass back through the same bead. Without adding beads, pass through the top beads of the edging, pulling tight so the beads close the end.

Step 8: Weave your thread through beads so you exit from a bugle at the bottom of the bead.

Step 9: Repeat Steps 5 and 7.

EMBELLISHING IDEA

Exit from one of the end beads in a three-stack round. Your thread should point away from the stack. *String a drop. Pass through the next end bead on the three-stack round. Pass through the rest of the stack and repeat from *. Continue working around the base bead, adding a total of 12 drops. Once you've made one round, continue around again, filling in the spaces.

Teresa Barrett, fiber artist and teacher, specializes in surface embellishments through fabric manipulation, dyeing, stitching, and beading. Some of her award-winning work can be seen at www.teresabarrett.com. She can be reached at warped8h@aol.com.

Garden of Delights

Anna Karena Tollin

Make this lively garden bead with leftovers from your stash. What a stunning centerpiece!

Materials
Cotton print fabric
Lightweight fusible interfacing
Varied sizes of seed beads
Assortment of Czech glass beads (round, leaves, flowers, drops, disks, etc.)
Large India glass cylinder bead
Size D beading thread
Hypo Tube cement

Notions
Size 12 beading needles
Scissors
Iron

Step 1: Cut the fabric wide enough to wrap the glass cylinder bead's circumference and overlap slightly; make the height 1" longer than the bead. Apply the interfacing to the wrong side of the fabric.

Step 2: Fold the raw edges under to fit the glass cylinder bead. Use the iron to make the edges crisp.

Step 3: Use any type of bead embroidery or fringe technique to sew beads to the right side of the fabric.

Work randomly or in a pattern. Keep a small width of space across one end bare so that you can make your overlap in Step 4.

Step 4: When most of the fabric is bead embroidered, wrap it around the glass cylinder bead and overlap the end. Stitch the fabric in place and embellish the seam so it can't be seen. The ends of the glass cylinder bead will be exposed.

Step 5: Use a small applicator tip to apply glue under the fabric to attach it to the glass cylinder bead. Allow to dry.

Anna Karena Tollin is a bead artist who lives in Minneapolis, Minnesota. Her work also appears in Beadwork Creates Necklaces *(Interweave Press, 2002). Contact her at annatollin@cs.com.*

Tips

STARTING A NEW THREAD

There's no doubt that you'll run out of thread as you work on your necklaces that use off-loom stitches. It's easy to begin a new thread. There are a couple of solutions. I prefer the first way because it's stronger.

Solution 1: Tie off your old thread when it's about 4" long by making a simple knot between beads. Pass through a few beads and pull tight to hide the knot. Weave through a few more beads and trim the thread close to the work. Start the new thread by tying a knot between beads and weaving through a few beads. Pull tight to hide the knot. Weave through several beads until you reach the place to begin again.

Solution 2: Here's how to end your old thread without tying a knot. Weave the thread in and out, around and around, through several beads and then trim it close to the work. Begin a new thread the same way, weaving the end of the thread in and out, around and around, and through several beads until you reach the place to begin again.

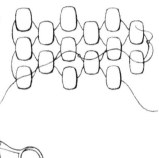

PASS THROUGH VS. PASS BACK THROUGH

Pass through means to move your needle in the same direction as the beads have been strung. Pass back through means to move your needle in the opposite direction.

TENSION BEAD

A tension bead holds your work in place. To make one, string a bead larger than those you are working with, then pass through the bead again, making sure not to split your thread. The bead will be able to slide along, but will still provide tension to work against.

Stitches

Brick stitch

Begin by creating a foundation
row in ladder stitch (see below).
String one bead and pass
through the closest exposed
loop of the foundation row.
Pass back through the same
bead and continue, adding one
bead at a time.

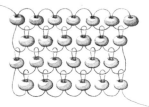

Back stitch

Back stitch (also known as "return stitch" and "running stitch").
Begin by passing the needle through the fabric, from wrong side
to right side, at the place where the first bead is to go. String a
bead and pass the needle back through the fabric to the left of
the bead. Bring the needle back through the fabric to the right
of the bead, pass back through the bead, and back down
through the fabric. Continue with one
backstitch per bead. You can sew up to
three beads per stitch by stringing three
beads and backstitching only through
the third as shown.

Ladder stitch

Using two needles, one threaded
on each end of the thread,
pass one needle through
one or more beads from
left to right and pass the other needle through the same beads
from right to left. Continue adding beads by crisscrossing both
needles through one bead at a time. Use this stitch to make
strings of beads or as the foundation for brick stitch.

Peyote stitch

This stitch can also be referred to as gourd stitch.

One-drop peyote begins by stringing an even number of beads to create the first two rows. Begin the third row by stringing one bead and passing through the second-to-last bead of the previous rows. String another bead and pass through the fourth-to-last bead of the previous rows. Continue adding one bead at a time, passing over every other bead of the previous rows.

Two-drop peyote is worked the same as above, but with two beads at a time instead of one.

Peyote stitch increase

Make a mid-project increase by working a two-drop over a one-drop in one row. In the next row work a one-drop peyote between the two-drop. For a smooth increase, use very narrow beads for both the two-drop and the one-drop between.

Peyote stitch increase

Peyote stitch decreases

To make a row-end decrease, simply stop your row short and begin a new row. To make a hidden row-end decrease, pass through the last bead on a row. Weave your thread between two beads of the previous row, looping it around the thread that connects the beads. Pass back through the last bead of the row just worked and continue across in regular flat peyote. To make a mid-project decrease, simply pass thread through two beads without adding a bead in the "gap." In the next row, work a regular one-drop peyote over the decrease. Keep tension taut to avoid holes.

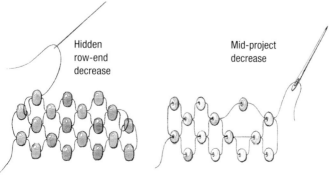

Hidden
row-end
decrease

Mid-project
decrease

Tubular peyote stitch

Begin by determining the diameter of the form you wish to cover. Thread an even number of beads to fit in a circle over this form. Make a circle by passing through all the strung beads twice more, exiting from the first bead strung. String one bead and pass through the third bead of the first round. String one bead and pass through the fifth bead of the first round. Continue adding one bead at a time, skipping over one bead of the first round, until you have added half the number of beads of the first round. Exit from the first bead of the second round. Slide the work onto the form. String one bead, pass through the second bead added in the second round and pull thread tight. String one bead and pass through the third bead added in the second round. Continue around, filling in the "spaces," one bead at a time. Exit from the first bead added in each round.

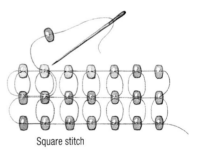

Square stitch

Begin by stringing a row of beads. For the second row, string 2 beads, pass through the second-to-last bead of the first row, and back through the second bead of those just strung. Continue by stringing 1 bead, passing through the third-to-last bead of the first row, and back through the bead just strung. Repeat this looping technique across to the end of the row. *To make a decrease,* weave thread through the previous row and exit from the bead adjacent to the place you want to decrease. Continue working in square stitch.

Square stitch

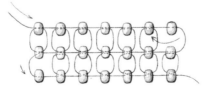

Square stitch decrease

Single-needle right-angle weave

The illustration refers to bead positions, not bead numbers.

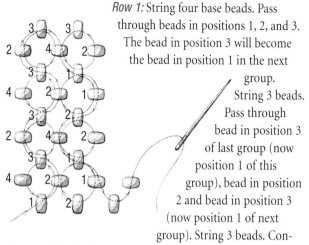

Row 1: String four base beads. Pass through beads in positions 1, 2, and 3. The bead in position 3 will become the bead in position 1 in the next group. String 3 beads. Pass through bead in position 3 of last group (now position 1 of this group), bead in position 2 and bead in position 3 (now position 1 of next group). String 3 beads. Continue working in this pattern until the row is to a desired length. In the last group, pass through beads in positions 1, 2, 3, and 4.

Row 2: String 3 beads. Pass through bead in position 4 of previous group and bead in position 1 of this group. String 2 beads. Pass through bead in position 2 of Row 1, bead in position 1 of previous group, and the beads just added. Pass through bead in position 4 of Row 1. String 2 beads. Pass through bead in position 2 of previous group and bead in position 4 of Row 1. Pass through first bead just added. String 2 beads. Pass through bead in position 2 of Row 1, bead in position 1 of previous group, and the first bead just added.

Row 3: Repeat Row 2.

Single-needle right-angle weave decrease

To make a row-end decrease, weave thread through the second bead added in the second-to-last group from the previous row. Begin the new row by stringing three beads. Pass back through the first bead added in the second-to-last group from the previous row. Pass through beads just added. Continue across row, adding two beads at a time.

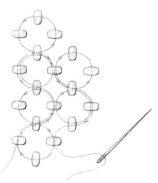

Double-needle right-angle weave

Using two needles, one on each end of the thread, string three beads and slide them to the center of the thread. Pick up a fourth bead, pass one needle through from left to right and pass the other needle through from right to left.

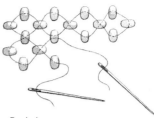

Begin here

Pick up one bead with each needle, then pick up one more bead and pass one needle through from left to right and pass the other needle through from right to left. Continue for desired length of row. To work next row, repeat as for first row, stringing new beads only onto the right thread and passing back through beads from first row with the left thread.

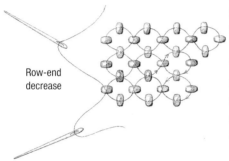

Row-end decrease

To make a row-end decrease, simply stop your row short and begin a new row.

Straight fringe

To make a straight fringe start it from a bead on the body of your piece. String the desired number of beads. Pass back through the second-to-the-last bead just strung. Continue back through all of the other beads just strung.

Kinky fringe

Anchor the thread in your fabric or beadwork base. String 15 to 20 beads. This is your base row. Skip the last bead and pass back through 6 to 8 beads. Pull the thread taut. String 6 to 8 beads. Skip the last bead and pass back through the beads just strung. Pass back through 6 to 8 beads of the base row, moving toward the top. Repeat Steps 2 and 3 until you reach the end of the base row.

Wireworked loop

Grasp one end of the wire with round-nose pliers. Holding on to the wire with one hand, gently turn the pliers until the wire end and wire body touch. Create a 90-degree reverse bend where they meet.

Wireworked spiral

To start a spiral, make a small loop at the end of a wire with round-nose pliers. Enlarge the piece by holding on to the spiral with chain-nose pliers and pushing the wire over the previous coil with your thumb.